HISTORIC
COMMUNITIES

18th Century Clothing

Bobbie Kalman

Toronto · Oxford · New York

Crabtree Publishing Company

Historic COMMUNITIES

Created by Bobbie Kalman

For my dear friend Vrajaprana

Writing team
Bobbie Kalman
David Schimpky

Illustrations
Antoinette "Cookie" DeBiasi
Barb Bedell (cover border)

Research
David Schimpky

Editors
David Schimpky
N-Lynne Paterson

Design and computer layout
Antoinette "Cookie" DeBiasi
Rose Campbell (cover mechanicals)

Separations and film
EC Graphics

Photograph credits
Courtesy of the Colonial Williamsburg Foundation:
title page, pages 5 (left), 6 (both), 7 (both), 8 (both),
9 (both), 10 (top), 12, 13 (top), 15 (bottom), 19,
20 (bottom two), 21 (bottom), 22 (both), 24 (top),
26 (top), 27, 28 (all)
Bobbie Kalman: pages 5 (top right), 10 (bottom),
13 (bottom), 15 (top), 18 (both), 20 (top), 21 (top),
24 (bottom), 29, 30 (both)
Jim Bryant: page 5 (bottom)
Fort George: page 26 (bottom)

Special thanks to
Cathy Grosfils (Colonial Williamsburg Foundation)
The students of Lakebreeze Elementary School
Dr. Nancy Smith, Robin Shaw, and Bernie Bajardi

Printer
Worzalla Publishing

Published by
Crabtree Publishing Company

350 Fifth Avenue	360 York Road, RR 4	73 Lime Walk
Suite 3308	Niagara-on-the-Lake	Headington
New York	Ontario, Canada	Oxford OX3 7AD
N.Y. 10118	L0S 1J0	United Kingdom

Cataloguing in Publication Data
Kalman, Bobbie, 1947-
  18th century clothing

(Historic communities series)
Includes index.
ISBN 0-86505-492-4 (library bound) ISBN 0-86505-512-2 (pbk.)
This book examines the clothing styles, accessories, and hygiene habits of men, women, and children in eighteenth century North America.

1. Costume - History - 18th century - Juvenile literature.
I. Title. II. Title: 18th century clothing. III. Series:
Kalman, Bobbie, 1947- . Historic communities series.

GT620.K34 1993   j391'.00971   LC 93-30701

Contents

Wool was pulled apart and fluffed with carding paddles.

Flax fibers were combed on a **hackle**.

Both wool and flax were spun on a spinning wheel.

A **loom** was used to weave cloth. Wool and linen were often woven together to make a cloth called **linsey-woolsey**.

New World fashions

Many Europeans sailed to the New World during the sixteenth and seventeenth centuries. They settled along the east coast of North America. Most of the colonists were from England, but settlers also arrived from France, Spain, Sweden, Germany, and Holland, bringing with them their different ways of dressing.

Clothes made at home

The new settlers made their homes in the wilderness. When the clothes they brought with them wore out, they had to make new ones. Fabrics were made from scratch. Wool, flax, and leather were the main materials used for making clothing.

Wool from sheep

Wool comes from fleece. Each spring farmers sheared the thick winter coats of sheep. The wool was cleaned of dirt, sticks, and burrs and greased to restore the oils lost during cleaning. It was then ready for carding, spinning, dyeing, and weaving.

From flax to linen

Flax plants were grown on most eighteenth century farms. The fibers of the flax plant were used to make **linen**. Since linen was lighter than wool, it was ideal for cool summertime clothing. The fine combed strands of flax were spun into thread and woven into linen cloth.

Leather

Animal hides were **tanned** and turned into leather, which was used to make clothing, bags, gloves, boots, and shoes. To tan leather, the colonists placed a hide in water and added oak

(above) Although cotton was grown in North America, it was made into cloth in England and shipped back to the colonies. The fluffy white part of the cotton plant was spun into thread and woven on a loom. Some plain homespun cotton was made in the southern colonies, but colorful, good-quality cotton cloth was expensive and only available in large communities. The dress in the picture was made from good-quality cotton fabric.

or hemlock bark. The bark released acid into the water. This acidic solution prevented the hide from rotting. The hide was left to soak in it for several months. When the leather was finally dried, it was stiff. To make it soft enough to wear, the colonists rubbed it with oil or animal fat.

(above) Sheep were shorn in the spring. Their wool was used by the settlers to make winter clothing.
(right) Leather was made from cow, deer, and sheep hides.

(top) In the eighteenth century most people were farmers. Farmers belonged to either the lower or middle class. Their working clothes were plain and practical.
(above) The clothing of the upper class was brighter, richer, and more colorful than those of the other classes. The suits and dresses worn by these wealthy men and women were made of expensive materials such as silk and brocade.

Different social classes

By the middle of the eighteenth century the small settlements along the east coast had grown into large towns and a class system formed among the people who lived there. The **lower class** was made up of laborers, servants, and poor farmers. They wore plain garments made of wool or linen in colors such as gray, brown, or white. The **middle class** consisted of artisans, professionals (such as doctors and lawyers), and farmers who owned some land. Middle-class people wore clothing that was modest, yet stylish. Their Sunday clothes were sometimes quite fancy.

People who owned a lot of land, traders, and those who were born into wealthy families belonged to the **upper class**. These people dressed in the most fashionable clothes, which were made from silk and other delicate materials.

*Dressmakers in Europe often sent dolls dressed in the latest styles to the colonies. These fashion dolls were called **moppets**. The wealthier colonists could order these clothes from Europe or have local tailors copy the fashions.*

(right) Artisans and laborers often wore leather breeches. Most of these people had only one or two outfits to wear, so they put aprons over their clothes to keep them from getting soiled or torn.
(below) Women who worked dressed simply and comfortably.

Working clothes

During the eighteenth century most men worked as farmers, artisans, or laborers. Their working clothes were practical, simple, and differed from occupation to occupation. It was easy to guess a man's profession from the clothes he wore. For instance, it was common for a doctor to wear a neat black suit and for a farmer to wear a broad, worn hat, a long, loose linen shirt, woolen breeches, and simple leather shoes.

Town workers

Artisans wore clothes that were suited to their work. For example, the leather worker used a heavy buckskin apron to protect his clothes from the tanning acid. The butcher also wore an apron as well as sleeve protectors. Laborers dressed in a plain shirt and leather breeches.

Women at home

Women raised children, cooked, carded wool, and did the spinning and weaving. They dressed simply, wearing linen or cotton in summer and wool in winter. Those who worked at home always wore an apron. A soft cap, called a **mobcap**, was the favorite head covering.

The servants of the rich

Wealthy people had servants do their work. In the homes of the very wealthy, male servants such as footmen and coachmen wore **livery** on special occasions. This household uniform consisted of a suit cut in the latest fashion. The colors were usually based on the family's coat of arms. Sometimes people thought servants in livery belonged to the upper class because their clothing was so fine.

(above) The coachman is dressed in fine livery.

Doctors and other professionals dressed in plain dark suits.

Shoes and boots

Many eighteenth century towns had resident shoemakers. Rural communities relied on visits from **itinerant** shoemakers who traveled from town to town. These artisans stayed at the homes of their customers while they made leather shoes and boots for the whole family.

Footwear for men

Men wore shoes made from cowhide or buckskin. There was no right or left shoe; both were identical. A few shoes were fastened with laces, but most shoes had large buckles. Some buckles were made from silver or gold, others of pewter or brass. Men's everyday shoes had square, rounded, or pointed toes and low heels. Wealthy men wore shoes called **pumps**, which had tiny heels and thin, delicate soles.

Eighteenth century shoes were identical. There was no left or right shoe. Most shoes had buckles, but a few shoes and boots were made with laces.

Footwear for women

Working women wore durable leather shoes, but wealthy women preferred more delicate shoes made of silk or linen. Some good-quality shoes were fashioned from fine, soft **kid leather**, which was made from the skin of young goats. Women's shoes usually had pointed toes and thick high heels. The shoe was fastened with a buckle. For riding, both men and women wore boots.

Women's dress shoes were made from silk, linen, or kid leather.

*Women wore **pattens** and **clogs** to protect their shoes from the mud. Men also wore clogs.*

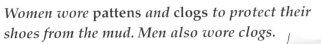

patten

clog

Men's shoes usually had buckles.

Wealthy men wore delicate pumps on formal occasions. Pumps looked like ladies' shoes.

These tall riding boots protected the knees.

*Heavy, stiff riding boots were called **jackboots**.*

*(below) Men put large boots, called **start-ups**, over their shoes to keep them from getting muddy.*

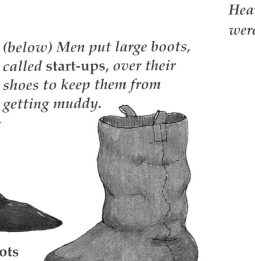

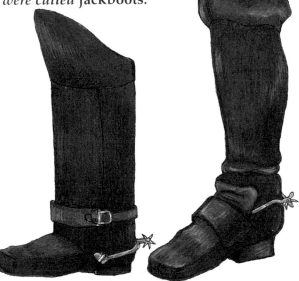

(above) **Highlow boots** *were light boots worn by working people.*

The woman on the left is wearing a petticoat and a fitted bodice with a stomacher and sleeve ruffles. Her guest is dressed in an open robe, which peeks out from under her **pelisse***. A pelisse is like a cloak, but it has slits or sleeves for the arms. She wears a* **calash** *to protect her tall hair style. A calash is a large hoodlike structure that can be folded down like the convertible top of an automobile. The servant's hairdo is much smaller, and her clothing is a lot less fancy.*

Women's fashions

In the eighteenth century, middle- and lower-class women wore simple cotton and linen dresses, but wealthy women wore beautiful gowns made from expensive materials. There were two main types of gowns: the **open robe** and the **closed robe**.

Fancy gowns were made up of different parts. The **bodice** was the upper part. The bottom half of the gown had two skirts: the **petticoat** and **overskirt**. Both reached below the ankle. The petticoat was worn beneath the overskirt and on top of another skirt called an **underpetticoat**. A **shift** was worn next to the skin. It was a cotton or silk undergarment that looked like a dress.

The open robe

The overskirt of the open robe was parted in front to reveal the petticoat. The petticoat was either the same material as the gown or made from a fabric that matched the gown. To keep the wearer warm in winter, the petticoat was quilted and stuffed with wool. Hoops were often worn underneath to give the skirt a domelike shape or to extend the hips sideways.

Many open robes had a tight bodice that was worn with a **stomacher**. This stiff panel was shaped like a triangle and was usually pinned to the front of the bodice.

The closed robe

The closed robe was much like the open robe, but the overskirt did not reveal the petticoat. A popular closed robe was called the **sack gown**. Its back featured loose pleats that started at the shoulders and reached down to the floor.

An open robe 1. bodice 2. stomacher 3. overskirt 4. quilted petticoat

closed robe (sack gown)

A skirt and long bodice (worn by the woman on the right) were worn on informal occasions.

13

1. painted fan 2. handkerchief 3. decorated apron 4. black winter mask and green summer half-mask 5. mobcap 6. buffon 7. nosegay 8. muff 9. gloves with and without fingers 10. assorted jewelry 11. reticule 12. pocketbook 13. embroidered stockings

Pockets were not sewn into dresses and gowns. A belt with single or double pockets was tied around the waist under the petticoat. Slits cut into each side of the skirts allowed this accessory to be used.

Muffs, masks, and ruffs

No outfit was complete without **accessories**. Accessories included neckwear, gloves, pockets, masks, pocketbooks, **reticules** (handbags), muffs, and watches.

Protection from the sun and wind

Suntans were not at all fashionable in these early times! Women wanted their skin to look as white and spotless as porcelain. They took great care to protect their faces from the sun and wind by wearing masks. Green silk masks prevented sunburns in summer, and black silk or velvet masks kept the face warm in winter.

Fashionable modesty

Many women did not feel comfortable wearing the low-cut dresses of the eighteenth century. For this reason, it became fashionable to wear kerchiefs and other neck accessories to cover up the neck and upper chest. Neckwear was also used to stay warm on cold days.

Some women wore folded handkerchiefs around their necks or covered themselves with a **modesty piece**, a lace-edged strip that was attached to the top of the neckline. Others used a **buffon**, a large transparent handkerchief that was draped across the chest. Frills, called **ruffs**, were also popular.

Fans for flirting

On a hot day, a fan was an important accessory for a woman. These portable air-conditioners were often decorated with beautiful designs. Some could be folded up, whereas others were rigid and held their shape. Their primary purpose was to keep a woman cool, but they were also used for flirting.

Protection for the hands

To keep their hands warm, women wore gloves or carried muffs. Women's gloves were made of leather or silk. They were almost always elbow length, although riding gloves were shorter. Muffs were short tubes of fur or other material in which the hands were placed for warmth.

Useful aprons

Aprons could be both fashionable and functional. Dress aprons were decorated and made of fine material. Everyday aprons were made of sturdy cloth. They kept skirts from getting dirty.

(top) Several accessories adorn this woman's outfit. She covers her neck with a buffon and her hands with gloves. A small watch is attached to her belt, and a green handbag that matches her dress hangs from her wrist.
(below) These women are both wearing aprons, hats, and shawls. The woman on the left warms her hands inside a muff. The one on the right has long leather gloves that do not cover her fingertips. This type of glove allows her to use her fingers.

Women's hair and hats

In the eighteenth century, a few women wore wigs, but most women styled their own hair. In the early 1700s, hairdos were simple. Women wore their hair loose or tied it back in a bun. One hair style was called the **tête de mouton**. The name is French for "sheep's head." This style had tight curls that resembled sheep's wool.

Early century hair styles were natural.

Elaborate hair styles

In the later part of the century, hair styles became taller and larger. These gigantic hairdos took hours to prepare and were often left in place for weeks. The hair was pulled up over wire supports or padding and was held in place with paste made from flour. Curls made of wool or thread were added over the ears. The hair was powdered and then decorated with colorful bows, ribbons, pins, feathers, and artificial flowers. Such a hair style could be more than three feet (one meter) high!

Sleeping with such a huge hairdo was not easy! Women covered their hair with a big net and sometimes placed their head on a wooden block while they slept. To save time and trouble, some

(below) The tête de mouton hairdo had tight curls. It was powdered to look gray.

These fancy hair styles must have been very uncomfortable!

(right) The hedgehog wig was fuzzy on top with long, loose curls at the neck.

The late-century bandeau style was soft and informal.

16

women wore wig versions of these hairdos, which could be taken off at night. Both the wigs and the hairdos carried unwelcome guests—fleas and lice!

Plain and fancy hats

Almost everyone in the eighteenth century wore a hat. Women's hats varied in size and style throughout the century. Soft caps were very popular. One of the most common was the mobcap. It was made of white linen or cotton and could be trimmed with satin or lace. It was usually worn indoors.

Farm fashions

More rigid hats were popular later in the century. Straw hats with low crowns and wide brims were called **bergère hats**. "Bergère" is French for "shepherdess." The style for this hat came from the wide-brimmed hats worn by women farmers. Fashionable women decorated these hats with ornaments and ribbon.

Later in the century, dress hats became larger and fancier. They were made of felt or straw and trimmed with feathers, pearls, and other ornaments.

soft cotton or linen cap

mobcap

cocked riding hat trimmed with fur

straw hat with a cap underneath

(above) bergère hat

(left) tall-crowned hat worn near the end of the century

(right) soft-crowned hat with lace curtains worn during the 1770s and 1780s

Underclothing

In the eighteenth century neither men nor women wore undershorts or underpants. Men wore their breeches next to the skin. Dress shirts were considered undershirts because they were covered up by a waistcoat and suit coat. Only the neck and sleeve ruffles were visible. Dress shirts were made of fine linen or cotton. Some wealthy men owned as many as fifty of these shirts!

Everyday shirts

Everyday shirts were often worn without a waistcoat or coat. They were made of cotton or linen and were tucked into breeches. The front of the shirt was open to the chest, but it could be buttoned at the neck.

(above) Men's shirts doubled as underwear. The shirt was tucked into breeches and covered a man's bottom. (below) Working women wore loose stays and bodices to allow them freedom of movement.

Shifts under dresses

Women wore a shift next to their skin. A shift was a loose cotton or linen dress that reached the knees and had elbow-length sleeves. It was worn beneath a dress and left on at night for sleeping.

Uncomfortable corsets

Another important part of a woman's under-clothing was the **stay**, or **corset**. It was made of cotton, linen, or silk and was stiffened with wire, whalebone, or wood. The stay was tightened with laces. Working women wore 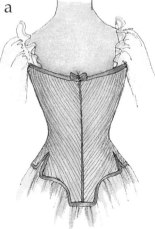 comfortable bodices and loose stays. Wearing a stay helped support a woman's back while she worked.

For a small-waisted look, women laced their stay very
tightly. Tight stays were both uncomfortable and
unhealthy, sometimes causing women to faint. Beneath
the stay was a shift. In the picture above, you can see a
pink shift with elbow-length sleeves and white lace trim.
Over the shift is a pink underpetticoat with a blue fringe.
A pocket is tied around the waist. The petticoat and
overskirt will be put on over the underpetticoat.

Pocket hoops *made a woman's stomach
look even flatter by widening the hips.*

This elegant frock coat decorated with silver braid would have been worn by a respected merchant, doctor or other professional.

Men's clothes

Men's suits consisted of stockings, breeches, a waistcoat, and coat. Everyday suits were made of linen or wool and came in simple colors such as brown, black, and dark blue. The suits of the wealthy were made of richly decorated silk, brocade, or velvet. These suits were worn at balls, concerts, and other special events.

Stockings

Stockings were an important part of a man's outfit. They covered his feet and calves. Fashionable men wore white or gray silk stockings, whereas working men used more durable and less expensive stockings made of linen or wool. Stockings were cut and sewn to fit a man's calves. They were held up above the knees with garters.

an English frock coat for everyday wear

a fancy formal silk suit

Breeches

Breeches ended just below the knee and were worn over stockings. They did not have a fly, as modern pants do. Instead, they had a square flap that buttoned up. They could be laced or buckled at the back for a better fit. In the early part of the century, men wore loose and comfortable breeches. Later on, tight breeches became fashionable.

Waistcoats

Waistcoats were sleeveless, collarless coats that looked very much like vests. They were worn beneath a coat. The front of the waistcoat was long and had one or two rows of buttons. It was usually made of the same material as the coat with which it was worn. The back of the waistcoat was much shorter than the front and was made of a less expensive cloth such as linen. Some waistcoats had sleeves. Servants, farmers, and artisans wore sleeved waistcoats under their coats when they worked outdoors in cold weather.

Coats

The styles of coats changed many times during the eighteenth century. Generally, coats were long and close fitting. They had many buttons and sleeves with large cuffs. Buttons, braiding, and brocade were used for decoration. In the early 1700s, coats were collarless but short standing collars were eventually added.

A popular style of coat was the **frock coat**. It had a turned-down collar instead of a standing one. There were two types of frock coats: the informal **English frock** worn for working, and the richly decorated **French frock**, which was reserved for formal occasions.

Banyans *were loose gowns made of patterned silk. They were worn inside the home in warm weather.*

During winter most men wore **greatcoats,** *which were heavy knee-length woolen coats. Men also wore cloaks similar to those worn by women, but men's cloaks did not have hoods.*

Men's accessories

Most eighteenth century men wore neckwear. A **cravat** was a linen scarf wrapped around the neck and tied at the front. The **stock**, another type of neckwear, was a high neckband fastened at the back of the neck. It made a plain shirt look fancy and fashionable. The stock was sometimes worn with a black tie called a **solitaire**. To keep their hands warm, men wore muffs or gloves. Men's gloves were usually made of leather or wool and could be long or short.

Hats for men

Men's hats were quite basic. **Cocked hats** were made of felt and came in brown or black. They were the most popular hats of the eighteenth century. The **tricorne** was a three-cornered

The men in both photographs are wearing cocked hats.

1. pocketbook
2. cravat
3. solitaire
4. stock
5. leather glove
6. spectacles
7. spectacle case
8. buckles
9. pocket watch
10. fob
11. snuff boxes
12. sword and
    sheath
13. cane

*Men carried pocket watches, **fobs**, and **snuff boxes**. A fob was an ornament attached to a watch chain. Snuff boxes were decorated boxes that contained a special type of tobacco that was inhaled through the nostrils.*

cocked hat. Farmers often wore practical **uncocked** felt hats that had a wide brim and low crown. These hats offered good protection from the sun and rain. At home, men wore soft caps or turbans.

Canes and swords

Upper-class men often carried beautifully decorated canes and swords mostly for the sake of fashion. The canes were intricately carved and inset with semi-precious stones.

uncocked
hat

tricorne

Wigs for men

Many people in the eighteenth century wore wigs, which were also called **periwigs** or **perukes**. Some gentlemen owned as many as ten! Wigs were heavy, hot, uncomfortable, and expensive. The most expensive ones were made of real human hair, but cheaper wigs, made of horsehair, goat hair, or thread, were also available. Some people had their own hair cut off and made into a wig. Wigs could be brown, black, or even blue, but the most popular colors were white and **grizzle** (gray).

Most men had their heads shaved regularly so their wig would fit better and feel more comfortable. There were several different styles of wigs, but the most common ones had one or two rows of curls over each ear and a tail called a **queue** hanging at the back of the neck.

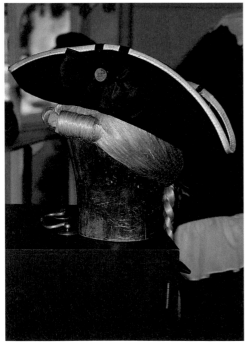

(top) The wigmaker has curled a gentleman's wig using clay rollers called buckles.
(above) This Ramillies wig has been cleaned, combed, curled, braided, and topped with a hat.

Wig styles

The **Ramillies wig** had a braided queue. The queue of the **bag wig** was held in a bag at the back of the head. The **cadogan wig** had a looped-up queue.

The **full-bottomed wig** was popular at the beginning of the 1700s. It was long and curly. The **hedgehog wig** was spiky, resembling a porcupine!

Large full-bottomed wigs were worn in the early 1700s.

Wig maintenance

A wig required regular maintenance. Before it could be worn, it had to be powdered. The person wearing the wig placed his face in a paper cone, and a servant dusted the wig with fine powder. Each week the wig was sent out to the barber or wigmaker to be cleaned and curled. It was cleaned with sand, combed on a hackle, and curled with heated clay rollers called **buckles**. Although wigs were cleaned, it was difficult to rid them of lice and fleas. Men who wore wigs had itchy heads!

bag wig

*(right) Wigs were powdered with **powder puffers**.*

cadogan wig with a looped-up queue

Ramillies wig with a braided queue

hedgehog wig

bob wig

25

Unhealthy habits

The people of the eighteenth century had different ideas about hygiene than we do. Some people washed their hands and face, but most people bathed only a few times each year. Those who cleaned themselves often were considered very strange by eighteenth century standards.

Bathing was difficult because there was no running water, and water had to be heated over the fire. Even if people could have bathed, they would not have done so because they believed that bathing robbed their skin of important oils that protected them from diseases.

(top) The people in this tavern do not seem concerned about body odor. It was part of eighteenth century life. (above) Homes did not have hot running water. Water was brought in from a well and heated over a fire.

Body odors

Lower-class people hardly ever changed or washed their clothes. Most of them only had one outfit for working and one for Sunday. Wealthy people didn't bathe much either, but their clothes were cleaner because they owned more outfits. As you can imagine, people must not have smelled very sweet, but they were used to body odor. Wealthy men and women sprinkled themselves with lavender water or wore small bouquets of flowers called **nosegays** to put a sweet smell near their nose.

People wearing plumpers often spoke with a lisp, which became fashionable.

Some women wore eyebrow "wigs" made from mouse fur.

Cosmetics

Upper-class men and women wore makeup. Makeup was used to look good, but it had another purpose. People used it to cover **smallpox** scars on their face. Smallpox was a serious disease that left many people with scar-covered skin. In order to hide these scars, people coated their face with white lead powder. Lead is extremely dangerous to one's health and caused sickness and even death. Another way to hide smallpox scars was to stick tiny silk or leather **patches** over them.

Smallpox patches came in many interesting shapes.

Teeth trouble

In the eighteenth century people worked hard at having a white smile. They used a variety of ingredients to clean their teeth. Acid, gunpowder, and sticks made from sea coral all had harmful effects. They wore away the enamel on teeth, causing them to decay and fall out. When people lost all their teeth, they replaced them with false teeth made of porcelain or ivory. Cork balls, called **plumpers**, were placed in the mouth to "plump up" the hollow cheeks caused by missing back teeth.

*Men and women covered their face with white lead powder and brushed **rouge** on their cheeks. Red salve, made from beeswax and red lead paint, was used to add color to the lips.*

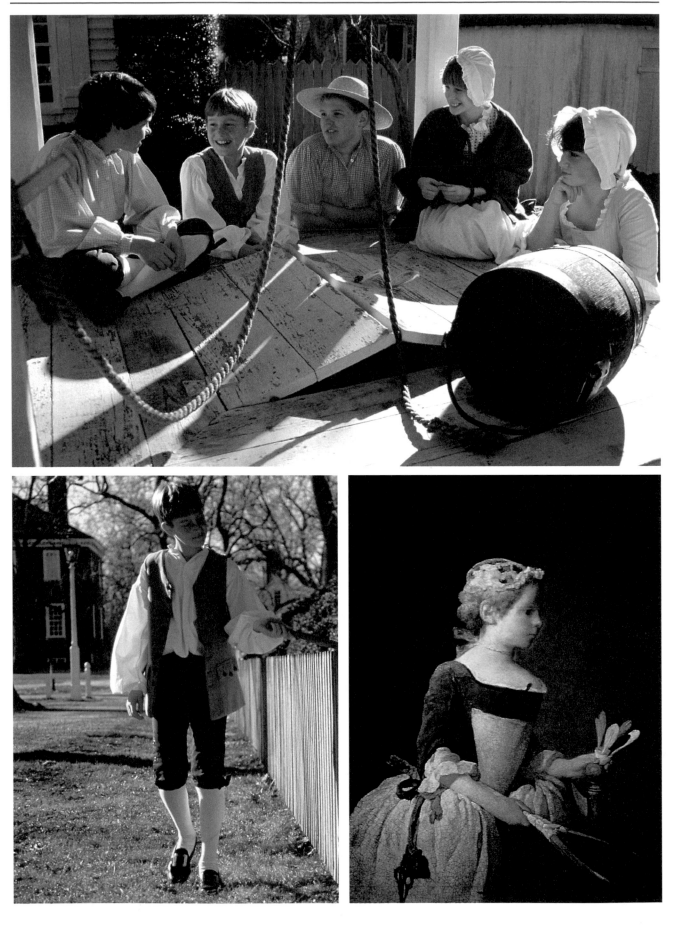

Children's clothing

Eighteenth century children were dressed much differently than children are today. Both boys and girls wore linen dresses until they were five or six years old. A young child's dress had a full skirt and tight bodice, but strings were attached to the back, not the front, of the bodice. The strings were used to hold on to the child when he or she was learning to walk.

Pudding for toddlers

Toddlers sometimes wore a **pudding**. A pudding was padding that was wrapped around the child's middle so that he or she could fall down while playing and not get hurt. Some toddlers also wore a soft padded hat that was a lot like a helmet. It was called a **pudding cap**, and it protected the child's head.

Dressing like little adults

After the age of six most children started dressing like their parents. Wealthy girls began wearing fancy silk dresses with stays. Many people believed that stays helped improve the posture of young women.

Upper-class boys wore fine waistcoats, breeches, and silk stockings. Many even wore wigs! The children of the middle and lower classes also wore clothes that resembled those worn by their parents.

(opposite page) Children wore small versions of their parents' clothing. Upper-class girls, such as the one in the bottom right painting, wore fancy gowns with stays. Lower- and middle-class children, as shown in the other pictures on these two pages, wore more casual clothing.

Toddlers who were learning to walk wore puddings to keep them from getting hurt when they fell down. Pudding caps protected their heads in case they fell or bumped into sharp objects.

Make your own costume

Dressing eighteenth century style is easy and fun. You can probably find all the clothes and accessories you need right at home. If you are a boy, you can start with long socks and short pants. If you do not have short pants, roll up a pair of long ones and tuck the ends into knee-length socks. A big, loose cotton shirt and vest will complete your outfit. You can make buckles from construction paper and stick them over dark leather shoes. (See illustration on page 23.)

Girls can wear long skirts, loose blouses, or fancy dresses that reach the floor. A shawl, apron, and a mobcap or straw hat are perfect accessories. Even a lace doily pinned on top of the head is suitable headwear. Ballet slippers and dress shoes with straps or buckles look similar to early footwear. If you have any problems, copy one of the outfits on this page or ask your friends to check their closets for items you may need.

(top) This class of children dressed up for a special historic occasion. They enjoyed putting their costumes together and wearing them.
(above) Robin found a cotton blouse, shawl, long skirt, and a mobcap in her mother's closet.

Glossary

accessory Something, such as a belt or purse, that is added to an outfit

artisan A skilled person, such as a tailor or carpenter, who makes and sells objects that he or she has made

bodice The part of the gown that covers the upper body

brocade A heavy cloth with a raised design

buckles Clay rollers that were heated and used to curl wigs

calash A hoodlike head covering that protected a woman's tall hairdo

cocked hat A hat with a turned-up brim

colonist Someone who lives in a colony

colony A territory that is controlled by a distant country

eighteenth century A period of one hundred years that began in 1701 and ended in 1800

fob An ornament attached to the end of a watch chain

garment An item of clothing

general store A small store that sold a wide range of items, including hardware, clothing, and food

greatcoat A man's overcoat

grizzle A popular gray color for wigs

hackle An instrument with steel teeth that was used for combing flax

itinerant Describing someone who travels from place to place

livery A fancy uniform worn by the servants of the very rich

loom A large machine that weaves thread or yarn into cloth

merchant A person who earns money by buying and selling goods

nosegay A small bouquet of flowers

pelisse A woman's cloak with a hood and sleeves or slits for the arms

periwig (or **peruke**) A wig

pewter A metal made from a mixture of tin and other metals

plantation A large farm where one type of crop is grown

pocket hoops Hoops that extended a skirt sideways

pocketbook A small folder or case used for carrying papers or money

porcelain A hard white substance made by firing and glazing clay

quilted Describing material consisting of two layers of fabric with a thick layer of cotton or wool in between

reticule A small handbag

settlement A recently settled community

seventeenth century A period of one hundred years that began in 1601 and ended in 1700

stay A woman's stiff underbodice that was laced tightly on her upper body; also known as a corset

stomacher A stiff panel that was attached to the front of the bodice

turban A head covering made by winding cloth around the head

underpetticoat A skirt worn beneath a petticoat

waistcoat A sleeveless coat buttoned up the front. It was worn under a coat.

whalebone A strong, thin material taken from the jaws of certain whales

Index

3 4 5 6 7 8 9 0 Printed in the USA 2 1 0 9 8 7 6 5 4